MEANING

of

MEOW

Edited by
Jeffrey Young

Author: Allegra Strategies
Design: John Osborne
Additional content: Anya Marco
Publisher: Allegra Publications Ltd

Visit our website:
meaningofeverything.com

All information was believed to be accurate at time of going to press. We have endeavoured to the best of our abilities to credit all quotes correctly and cannot be held responsible for any omissions or oversights. We thank all the quotees and individuals who have collectively contributed to this book, either directly or indirectly. The content of this book has been gathered from various sources in the public domain. Some of the quotes have been edited to achieve the overall objectives of the publication.

Published by *Allegra* PUBLICATIONS Ltd © 2015

Walkden House, 10 Melton Street, London, NW1 2EB, UK

Dedicated to
Barney, Mattie & Little Cat

One kind word can change
someone's entire day.

Start each day with a smile (and get it over with).

GARFIELD

I left my husband.
The cat was allergic.

Cat's motto:

No matter what you've
done wrong, always try to
make it look like
the dog did it.

Hey human.
Why are you taking
a photo of me?

The problem with cats is they have the same look, whether they see a butterfly or an axe murderer.

Some people say that cats
are sneaky, evil, and cruel.
True, and they have many
other fine qualities as well.

STEPHEN BAKER

Cats rule the world.

JIM DAVIS

The more people I meet,
the more I like my cat.

If a cat spoke,
it would say things like:
'Hey, I don't see the
problem here.'

ROY BLOUNT

Learn from your
parents' mistakes.
Use birth control or
get a couple of cats.

The best things in life aren't things.

These aren't my thoughts,
they're my cat walking
on the keyboard.

There is no snooze button on a cat who wants breakfast.

Cats:

The real reason you're late

for work today.

I was married by a judge.
But I should have asked for
a jury or a cat.

GROUCHO MARX

Kittens are angels
with whiskers.

I'd like mornings better if they started later.

GARFIELD

Most beds sleep up to six cats. Ten cats without the owner.

STEPHEN BAKER

If a dog jumps in your lap, it is because he is fond of you; but if a cat does the same thing, it is because your lap is warmer.

ALFRED NORTH WHITEHEAD

Researchers have discovered that dogs can comprehend a vocabulary of 2,000 words, whereas cats can only comprehend 25 to 50. No one ever asks how many words researchers can comprehend.

There are no ordinary cats.

COLETTE

A cat's life is hard,
then you nap.

Be a Fruit Loop
in a wonderful world
of Cheerios.

Too many cats?
Your neighbours forget
your last name and start
referring to you as
"you know, the cat people."

KATHIE FREEMAN

MEOW =
Make
Everything
Officially
Wonderful

Never feed your cat
anything that doesn't
match the carpet.

Kittens can happen

to anyone.

PAUL GALLICO

If cats could talk, they wouldn't.

NAN PORTER

I love cats because I enjoy my home; and little by little, they become its visible soul.

JEAN COCTEAU

I purr, therefore I am.

Too many cats?
For Mother's Day last
year the kids pooled their
money and bought you an
electric cat brush.

KATHIE FREEMAN

The idea of calm
exists in a sitting cat.

JULES RENARD

There is no more intrepid explorer than a kitten.

JULES CHAMPFLEURY

Oh, if I offended you with my opinion, you should hear the ones my cat keeps to himself.

Cats can work out
mathematically the exact
place to sit that will cause
most inconvenience.

PAM BROWN

It's kind of fun
to do the impossible.

WALT DISNEY

Cats know how we feel.
They don't care,
but they know.

If cats looked like frogs
we would realise what
cruel and nasty bastards
they really are.

TERRY PRATCHETT

Some people have cats and go on to lead normal lives.

A meow massages
the heart.

STUART M^CMILLAN

Purring: An automatic safety device to deal with an overflow of happiness.

Cats have a scam going –
you buy the food, they eat
the food, they go away;
that's the deal.

EDDIE IZZARD

Happiness isn't getting
all you want. It's enjoying
what you have.

Stop focusing on what you have to lose and instead on what you have to gain.

A bird sitting in a tree is not afraid of the branch breaking. Because it trusts in its own wings.

Cats are like music. It is foolish to try to explain their worth to those who don't appreciate them.

The cat loves fish,
but she's loath
to wet her feet.

I couldn't update my
Facebook status.
My cat ate my mouse.

Naps are for old people.
That's why I am taking a
horizontal pause period.

GARFIELD

Nobody cares if you are miserable, so you might as well be happy.

Dogs have owners.
Cats have staff.

Cats only pretend to be
domesticated if they think
there's a bowl of milk
in it for them.

ROBIN WILLIAMS

Sit down, said the cat.
Let me tell you a story.
Once upon a time,
I ate your hamster
this morning.

You know when people see a cat's
litter box, they always say,
'Oh, have you got a cat?'
Just once I want to say,
'No, it's for visitors!'

Time spent with cats is never wasted.

MAY SARTON

Gentle eyes that see so much,

paws that have the quiet touch.

Purrs to signal "all is well"

and show more love than words could tell.

Graceful movements touched with pride,

a calming presence by our side.

A friendship that takes time to grow,

small wonder why we love them so.

Dogs come when they are called. Cats take a message and may or may not call you back later.

People that don't like cats
haven't met the
right one yet.

DEBORAH A EDWARDS

Hand over the catnip
and no one will get hurt.

There is something about the presence of a cat... that seems to take the bite out of being alone.

LOUIS J CAMUTI

When life puts you in tough situations, don't say 'Why me?' Just say 'Try me!'

GARFIELD

I hate being bi-polar.
It's really awesome.

Cats are connoisseurs of comfort.

JAMES HERRIOT

They don't keep you on a
leash because they want
you to run away
– said the dog.

If there were to be a universal sound depicting peace, I would surely vote for the purr.

BARBARA L DIAMOND

I would love to go out
with you, but I have to stay
home and brush my cat.

Any conditioned cat-hater
can be won over by any
cat who chooses to make
the effort.

PAUL COREY

Happy is the home
with at least one cat.

ITALIAN PROVERB

Sufferin' Succotash!

SYLVESTER THE CAT

I was a grumpy cat
before it was cool.

GARFIELD

Warning:
Children who misbehave
will be given a double
espresso and a kitten.

When the cat's away,
the mice will play.

No matter how much cats fight, there always seem to be plenty of kittens.

ABRAHAM LINCOLN

I wish I could write
as mysterious as a cat.

EDGAR ALLAN POE

Old cats mean young mice.

The cat shuts his eyes
while he steals the cream.

Everything I know I learned
from my cat: When you're hungry,
eat. When you're tired, nap in a
sunbeam. When you go to the vet,
pee on your owner.

GARY SMITH

Be happy for this moment.
This moment is your life.

Often the cats who need the most affection are the ones that are the most difficult to love and scratch you when you're trying to pet them.

I have cats instead
of children. I would rather
ruin the sofa, than
ruin my life.

Sleeping together is a euphemism for people, but tantamount to marriage with cats.

MARGE PIERCY

Authors like cats because they are such quiet, lovable, wise creatures, and cats like authors for the same reasons.

ROBERTSON DAVIES

You know, there are times when it's a source of personal pride to not be human.

CALVIN AND HOBBES

The imagination is man's power over nature.

WALLACE STEVENS

What part of 'Meow' don't you understand?

For a man to truly
understand rejection,
he must first be ignored
by a cat.

'Meow' means 'woof' in cat.

GEORGE CARLIN

One day I was counting
the cats and I absent-
mindedly counted myself.

BOBBIE ANN MASON,
SHILOH AND OTHER STORIES

What greater gift than the love of a cat.

CHARLES DICKENS

To err is human,
but to purr is feline.

ROBERT BURNS

We have three cats.
It's like having children,
but there is no
tuition involved.

RONALD REAGAN

There is, incidentally,
no way of talking about
cats that enables one to
come off as a sane person.

DAN GREENBERG

You can never start a
new chapter of your life if
you keep re-reading
the last one.

Cats and their owners are on a private, exclusive loop of affection.

SLOANE CROSLEY

Just watching my cats can make me happy.

PAULA COLE

You can teach a cat to do anything it wants to do.

I had been told that the training procedure with cats was difficult. It's not. Mine had me trained in two days.

BILL DANA

A dog accepts you as
the boss, but a cat wants
to see your CV.

Cats seem to go on the principle that it never does any harm to ask for what you want.

JOSEPH WOOD KRUTCH

These are my principles,
and if you don't like them...
well, I have others.

GROUCHO MARX

Climb your way to the top.
That's why the drapes
are there.

Happiness is a journey, not a destination.

Always give generously.
A small bird or rodent left
on the bed tells them
I care.

A black cat crossing your path signifies that the cat was going somewhere.

GROUCHO MARX

Those who were seen
dancing were thought to
be mad by those who could
not hear the music.

FRIEDRICH NIETZSCHE

I tawt I taw a puddy tat...

TWEETY

Two mice are eating a movie film roll at a cinema when one says to the other, 'this movie is good, but the book was better.'

As anyone who has ever been around a cat for any length of time well knows, cats have enormous patience with the limitations of the human kind.

CLEVELAND AMORY

The purity of a person's heart can be quickly measured by how they regard cats.

It's really the cat's house –
we just pay the mortgage.

The smart cat
doesn't let on
that she is.

There are few things in
life more heart warming
than to be welcomed
by a cat.

Floyd was all set for a lap dance and then he remembered what the vet removed.

Sometimes all I need
are your arms around me
and you telling me
it's going to be OK.

Today is a good day
to have a good day.

The unkittened life is not worth living.

SOCRATES

My husband said it was
him or the cat...
I miss him sometimes.

Catastrophe.
The feeling of being
without your cat.

Be the person that your cat
thinks you are.

Way down deep, we're all
motivated by the same
urges. Cats have the
courage to live by them.

JIM DAVIS

Thousands of years ago, cats were worshipped as gods. Cats have never forgotten this.

Enjoy the little things in life, for one day you may look back and realise they were the big things.

Every sixty seconds you spend upset is a minute of happiness you will never get back.

There comes a time when you either have to choose between turning a page or closing a book.

Don't wait for
the perfect moment.
Take the moment
and make it PURRfect.

The difference between a cat and a lie is that a cat has only nine lives.

MARK TWAIN

Never look down on anybody unless you're helping them up.

JESSE JACKSON

Never trust a man, who
when left alone with a tea
cosy... doesn't try it on.

BILLY CONNOLLY

We have a theory that cats are planning to take over the world, just try to look them straight in the eye... yup, they're hiding something!

DOG FANCY

People who hate cats
will come back as mice
in their next life.

Notes

Ideas

Dreams

Schemes

Notes

Thoughts

Ideas

Dreams

Plans

Thoughts

Ideas

Dreams

Schemes

Plans

Notes

Thoughts

Ideas

Dreams

Plans

MORE FROM ALLEGRA PUBLICATIONS

The Meaning of Coffee

The Meaning of Wine

The London Coffee Guide

The New York Coffee Guide

The Vienna Coffee Guide

The Belgium & Netherlands Coffee Guide

The London Cheese & Wine Guide

Great Cake Places

Allegra
PUBLICATIONS